Reveries, In Passing

AF624622

Kim Przystupa

BookLeaf Publishing

Presentation by *BookLeaf Publishing*

Web: www.bookleafpub.com

E-mail: info@bookleafpub.com

ISBN: 9789357449045

First edition 2022

Elation/Despair

I find mania
to be blissful
like sun, or
blooms of pure white.
Atom bombs
that bathe innocents
in divine yet cruel light.
A broad radial burden
on those closest, it is shared.
What of patience and empathy -
can't stand that dull fare.

On the flipside
comes weight.
Thin dilution of agency
with backwash of anxiety.
Past oblivion sleep
obligations drift by.
A petri dish of dish slime
a fast friend to fruit fly.
Monologues of I should
and "tomorrow I'll retry,"
(this in-truth, a self-lie.)

Take two

deep breaths

and release.

Within cyclical tides
and one corner of mind
is an ideal agar
for the culture of self-pity.
Despite a sample size of 1I find, that
recognition and acceptance
of self-loathing
is a pivot, for creating
the mental breathing space
sufficient for mechanical,
constructive trickery.

Like re-defining the phrase
"driven to distraction,"
there is syrupy, meta-pleasure
in replacing one feeling
with concrete satisfaction.

Took Too Much

Voices of evil
  I'd kept them at bay
    can't tell if they're real
  psychedelics in-play
Enter blue doorways, and portals
  a splintering brain
    appeal to my echos
  pull together I say
All-seeing eye in the desk
  black pen mark, now astray
Desperate washing of hands
  "I'm ok, I'm ok"
    the sink overflows
  questionnaire yields insane
If tomorrow I'm one piece
  to dear God I shall pray

Medicine

remembrance of evening
 of grief and redemption (1)
rock music of ages
 sampled sound truly ageless (2)
straight-arrow percussion
 released towards the future (3)
virtuoso of youth (4)
 rumination of age (5)
modern reformulation
 skyscrapers of glass (6)
arpeggi nostalgia
 decisive, urgent attack (7)
oak chimes and sliced spoons
 withdrawn from the past (8)
sharp snares that explode
 raining shards from the sky (9)
subterranean bass
 emerald glint in your eye (10)
atmosphere up in flames
 a reflection of mind (11)
rhythm like a machine
 hi-hats glinted with shine (12)
lofi electric guitar
 the adventure of life (13)
piano synth reverb
 venetian boat ride (14)

bankroll for the bitches
        coat of diamonds and ice (15)
old grills from the projects
        gold blood from that life (16)
kanye just be kanye
        plow past thick dissent, (17)
ride onwards, through strife.

-

1. Four Tet - Evening Side
2. Shlohmo - Rock Music
3. Djrum - Thank You
4. Glenn Gould - Goldberg Variations: Aria (1955)
5. Glenn Gould - Goldberg Variations: Aria (1981)
6. Lang Lang - Goldberg Variations: Aria (2021)
7. Kelly Lee Owens - Arpeggi
8. Shlohmo - Things I Lost
9. Shlohmo - Beams
10. Deft - Emeralds
11. Feral - In Flames
12. Machinedrum - Stone Age
13. Unknown Mortal Orchestra - That Life
14. Saloli - Barcarolle
15. BROCKHAMPTOM - BANKROLL
16. Blood Orange - Gold Teeth
17. Kanye West - Everything We Need

Beachside

it is fleeting

and so precious

with or without partner
an inky feeling of being
deeply ok
with marble-blue solitude.

absent of sorry

just admiration -
for aqua wildflowers
glazed with cloudcover
and woody detritus
washed in cool waters
from things we felt fondness for
but can't quite remember

that blend naturally into
the grain of old sand

seated in present
we observe at a distance
sift silently
          allowing
loam hues to drift
and depart from one hand

once-sharp edges
become feathered silt
internally layered
of implicit identity;
formations of land.

First Gen.

During my last visit
I found a photo:
one of my mother.
A grainy pair of
muddy flats -
barriers
separating tiny feet
from steps of dirt.
Despite decades
her eyes
transmitted an expression
that I could recognize.

They immigrated
separately, and alone
in the 80's, against a backdrop
of cold
war uncertainty.

They were reticent
about their circumstances
yet with time, I gleaned enough
to recognize, implicit marks
traced by hardship;

and of honorable
abject scarcity.

My father worked
as if hunted.

I resented
for many years,
a struggling, and imperfect,
loving,
pair of immigrants; for accumulated
superficial misalignments.
Naive judgments that
withered, in the light of
their exhausted
sleeping figures.

Homelife was a gift

long-dated
of books, and education.

for my father
was not present.
at his only
brother's funeral.
He had every right
to bitterness.

Yet his voice
on the phone
was warm, and
placid.

Scientific Wet Dreams

chuck's art
machine learning
and biology
they must be connected
if not in reality
then at least:
in dreams, and mind fuckery.

just a little fire flickering,
wisps of soft smoke
from fine fantasy.

Shame

being shameless
or just shame
the word is so loaded
but overall what could be better?
or what could be worse, to inflict on another?
consider
shame as a blunt tool we use
in place of a suture
to make up for our lack
of clear plans for the future.
what is its use?
suppression!
of black fears, the unknown
like closing our eyes
in deep ocean water.
of lovecraftian creatures
so huge in our minds.
yet the ocean is wide!
one vast, hidden ecosystem
truly brimming with life.

Consent

Maybe one origin is consent.
Maybe years ago, or just prior.

Consent.

Your parents, and peers:
did they ask?
did you feel
violated,
small,

less human?

What if
you were asked?
and why didn't they ask?
and why didn't I ask?

We all have mixed reasons
which aren't a small matter
but at least one tenet
of all living beings

is consent.

Consent boils down to respect
for other egos, for threats.
For something with a will of its own
that will show you your flaws
and expose imperfection.

Maybe due to biology
this feels right:
the way it should be
the way we wished it would be.

Perhaps most importantly:
the way it can be.

Like fruit trees
we nurture scents of the future
for crisp fruit that gets sweeter.
Built on old family recipes
we improve
generationally.
Rework soil and old legacy,
one day yielding
that splendid
peach tea.

Hail Mary

Not being a homewrecker
seemed like the right avenue,
you know, just sort of
the right thing to do.

So in contrast to the past
last week I found myself
on good behavior.
Holding back due to karma
and all of that jazz.

Till finally i asked
where they stood with their other
and after, i knew:
they were out of my grasp.

Rather than peel back
an uncovered corner
            excavate some stale chemistry
simply asking felt fair
to us, and the phantom +1.

One plus
was the lightness
not quite giddy
more like …
sweet-and-sour self-esteem.

I guess in the interim
instead of a honeymoon phase
I'll just fill it
with some other thing.

Regress to the mean
            at least temporarily
it's not bad -
this peppery-plush nicotine.

A Bag

An old tattered orange backpack.
The right zipper cannot be shut.
It is too small for fat laptops.
Even as the label peels off the front,
It will not be replaced by another rucksack.
There's none as good that exists.

It has adventures wherever it goes.
Whether it is walking or out running
On mountains, or the bottom of valleys,
Through torrential tributes or incendiary heat.
The bag's integrity was kept around the world.
It is a steady companion on life's journeys.

This bag, containing an assortment of things.
Carrying a world inside as it travels:
A broken plug to an archaic technology;
Coarse specs of baking soda to kill odor;
Dry blood, damp sweat, gravel from sports;
Each a moment of a life being lived.

The only thing that works is a clasp.
It buckles firmly around the breast;
Some cheap approximation of an embrace.
A synthetic hold from plastic and fiber straps,
A reminder of fond times since past,
A soft touch in the next struggle to face.

There are better backpacks out in the world.
Ones without holes, with working zippers.
Others with more capacity and better design.
Yet this one remains despite wear and tear.
To remember my friend who used to own it.
It’s a carried, cherished orange memory of mine.

A Collection of Woes

(1) Please, Don't:
Laying on the bottom step of home,
Curled up like a fetus in the womb,
Broad shoulders, six feet tall.

Having traversed around the globe.
Having contended with great athletes.
Having transcended fields of science.

Yet there is only one thing on the mind:

Please do not go.

Please do not leave me.
For God sake, don't do this.
For all the world,
don't go!
I can't fight it anymore!
it repeats,
It's repeated,
it's repeating.

Please, please, please,
Please don't go.
Compressed into a point in the mind.

A singular point at the core of being:

Please don't leave me,
Please don't go.

No more walls,
No more rationale ideals,
No more philosophy.
Just Please,
Don't go.

Another round of weeping,
Cradled in a fetal position,
At the base of a step.

No equations to solve the problem,
There is no solution,
No comforting words,
No resolution.

Letting out what needs to be let out.
Squeezing harder to let go,
Over something lost.

Just the steady stream of tears,

Of a broken, sad, man.

(2) The Importance of Touch:

There's a memory of her in my mind,
the perfect idea of what a partner can be.
She's with me, by my side,
holding my hand.

She's gone now.
I'm high on some street drug,
crying again,
Not feeling whole anymore.
There is nothing now,
Remembering she used to be here.
That she used to hold my hand.

A phantom knife is held against the throat.
Waiting, always waiting to strike,
Waiting to materialise,
To be no more a phantom.
What used to be warm embraces,
What used to be joy.
It's gone now,
Because she's not holding my hand.

(3) Cycles of Sorrows:

It sweeps over without warning,
The anger and then the tears.
Again and again and again.

It's better now,
Than eight months ago,
Yet it still keeps happening.
A piece of him died,
But now it's time to try and fix it.

The images are violent,
The visions never end well.
Try as one might to keep it away,
It returns,
The anger and then the tears.

(4) I Miss You:

Oh how many different ways,
On how many different days,
Can I continue to say I miss you?
That I dream to once again kiss you?

To hold your slender frame in my arms;
Both naked in bed and clothed in the yard;
To hear you worry on about your work;
To see your disgust when I am being a jerk.

To kiss your soft head of hair black as night;
To kiss your soft cheeks after we fight;
To be glad having you by my side;
Those were the days that I felt most alive.

So what else is there that rhymes can say?
Here I go again, missing you today.

Howling Winds

The wind's howling outside tears against
people's skin.
Despite the thick jacket there's still chilling
across the air.
These winds are not to be defied, humbled are
those who dare!
These fools that think against the elements
they'd win.

Invisible needles are pressing into rosy cheeks.
The roar of nature's voice sounds all around.
It swirls on high across a wintry small town.
One thinks that things will continue to be so
bleak.

Yet fear not yonder traveller in the white snow!
Fasten your coat closer, adjust your scarf!
Head towards a warmer place from the chilling
cold!

Trudge on through the winter towards your
home.
Keep spirits lest the terror of weather tear you
apart.
You can withstand frigid seasons despite death's
hold.

Hypocrite

Most free verse poetry is:
complete crap.
Structural madness,
with cryptic messages!
Utter,
Complete,
Nonsense.
With grandiose,
stringing of words
together.
In odd
shapes or
gramm-
atical splatter!
Such poetry is the dollop of paint
On a white canvas,
That sells for 10,000 dollars.
Objectively,
no skill at play,
No artistry!
What.
So.
Ever.
Yet people still find value in it!
What
A
Travesty.

Let Pain Sow Growth

May gods transform these pains into progress.
Although there is a hollowed shell of man,
These tears transform seeds into more not less.
Let grief's weight cause strength to grow where we stand.

Let this mind and hands bring purpose to this world!
To create things that might touch the souls of people.
May we bring friends in for new joys to unfurl.
To remind the spirit that we are more than sheep still!

Today, I'm not the man I need to be,
My actions are mockerys to goodness.
Yesterday a fool, but I am still not yet prepared.

Let this be time of joy for those en masse to see.
Tired as we are, tis not time to go into pressured rest.
To show, the man she'd love was always there.

Persian Queen

My Persian queen whom I would worship so,
With raven hair beneath your Golden crown.
Years pass, we met, that seems so long ago.
We talked and laughed in foreign towns.

Your charming face and bright brown eyes,
Your smile, which came with it, such lovely sounds,
But present day, we are not near enough insight.
I dreamed a day where you'd be here in white a gown.

Off you marched claiming other people's lands.
Rebuild your kingdom of Iran far overseas.
To leave me here, in freezing lands, with empty hands.

Oh please, my queen, it is you whom I bend the knee.
Let me be yours to lead, to be at your command.
Instead, you do me death as one who is nobility.

Rat King

One:
How could people condemn free birds to inside metal cages?
The birds are meant to fly on air currents, amazing us.
Eloquent accents to heaven above with their plumage fluttering in the sky,
Rainbows of colorful, flashing wings soaring overhead on high.

You look to the blue sky above breathing in fresh, crisp air.
You are a rat, with a bum leg, so you stay in sewers.
Among the trash of discarded items of the average people,
Nibbling on decaying food that's got a wretched horrid reek still.

Go on! Fight tooth and claw killing rats to rise to the top of your rat hill!
Being king of the rats does not get you closer to the sky still.
All the bubonic plague you carry makes you more of a menace.

Cling on to your rat dreams of flying in the clouds as you live in rat ignorance.

It doesn't matter how much you pray to rat elder Jesus.
Your days are better spent searching for blue, moldy cheeses.
Go drown yourself in toxic waters to spare the world of the filth just like yourself.
If not, rat king, accept that fate hath doomed you to rats life and nothing else.

Two:
One day while the rat king was gnawing on a scrap, carcass dinner.
He heard a high pitch squawk in the bushes with an enamoring twitter.
The rat king is afraid, but he prepares to investigate the potential threat.
His claws and fangs ready to kill a foe which has not been identified yet.

He's rushing through the brush prepared to kill threats to the rat king's ways.
Against the rat-killer-instincts, he's stopped by what is embraced by his rat gaze.
A broken winged dove who has been cast down from the rat's sky heaven.

Bloodlust has left the rat; his mind's a fog. What should a rat king do then?

Along comes other hungry rats looking to eat a fresh bird snack.
Rat king snaps back, on the attack, to kill the encroaching rat pack.
The king sinks jagged teeth in the lead rat's jugular vein.
The king pulls visceral from his victim who won't move ever again.

The rats swarm on the king, but stumble over their fallen leader.
They trample a blood-stained mess that is the newest worm feeder.
They're being slain by a red eyed demon who imparts final judgement.
By the end, the king's eye is gouged, but the bird is in need of tweet-ment.

Three:
The king nurses the bird to health by fulfilling all her bird needs.
He trades his winter stores to other rats to provide her birdseed.
King knows of a doctor who could help set her wing bones.

Rat king cajoles the doctor to help as a favor from long ago.

The doves peril began when she accidentally crashed into a building.
She spiraled from the sky like heavy weighted gold bullion.
While the dove is recovering she tells stories of the sky and what it's like to fly.
It's exhilarating, entertaining, and exonerating.
Up there's to be alive.

The king lost half a tail taking risks to help his beloved dove out.
She soothes his pain with songs while the king squeeks aloud.
She's chirping on and on about why rat king is so great to be doing this.
She's overjoyed from rat king's help despite the sacrifice and risk.

The day comes the dove's wing is healed so that she can soar again.
The rat king's delusion is shattered. He can't comprehend it is the end.
You can't go back to a rat life knowing the story songs of the avian clans.
She leaves you with nothing but "thank you".
You're alone in the rat badlands.

A shell of the rat that you were before running
into that damaged bird that was almost dinner.
An empty eye socket, no tail, missing teeth, and
no food to make it through the winter.
The fallen king's reward is a squawk of thanks
for having saved her.
The dumb rat dies for having gone against rat
nature.

Shades of People

The first seems just like yesterday:
Reflective lense aviators!
You felt like a cool movie star.
It did not last long though.
They got jealous,
When the prescription lenses came,
So aviators had to go.

The next pair was in California:
a cheap wood-plastic frame!
They were no-name brand,
Good for the west coast sun.
Then there was that one stressful night.
They snapped under pressure.

We had a fling with one in Nevada:
A red, white and blue patriot!
They were nice, but the boys didn't like em.
They got lost in the desert sand.
We never saw them after that.
It did not even last 4 days.

There was an alright lime green pair from work.
We walked the pride parade,
We saw San Francisco.
She was a lot of fun,
But she had a screw loose,
And I was too lazy to address it.
Eventually, things fell apart.

These were just the memorable ones.
So many shades over years,
So many different sunglasses.
A box of forgotten ones on the dresser,
Not even worth mentioning.

The latest pair is a rainbow,
People seem to like the colors,
I seem to like the colors.
The hinge screw is loose again,
But I have a screwdriver,
To fix the issue.
I'd rather not lose them.
I'd rather keep this pair for a lifetime.
I've tried enough shades to know when one is a keeper.

The Self-Righteous

We have done it!
We have done it!

We captured the witch of our city!
Bind their body tightly against the pyre;
A tall stick collection that burns away evil,
Burn the entity of sin who tempts man's desire.

Perhaps the evidence of witchcraft is shady at best.
Perhaps none of us know first-hand of their witch-ways,
But a random passerby claimed witness to witchcraft,
So that's enough to burn them at sunrise today.

Witchcraft comes predicated by infallible sins:
They spread blasphemy against our God above.
They enchant our good people into monsters.
Their thoughts differ from us, which is evil enough!

We living people know these crimes are sinful.
We living saints carry the strictures from intransient God.
All past people were sinners who prayed to the devil.
Only modern white hot flame can right the world's wrongs!

Yes, we are the paladins of purity of earth!
We stamp out demons, witches, and ghouls no matter how big or small.
We cleanse the world not with forgiveness, but by the punishing iron rod.
We have God's fury behind us to justify our actions after all!

So hark modern day templars, let's get all the witches!
Let's tear down their lives because our goodness is perfected.
Let's murder them with all the kind love in our hearts!
Be deaf to their evil words which we know are misdirected.

Tie up the modern witches securely to the pyre!
We are justified in burning away evil of any size!
Let our searing goodness rise to the heaven we no longer pray to!
When the murdering is done, only our good people will survive!

Thoughts of Stories

A bored mind reflecting on a lazy Friday night.
Wondering about many things in stories,
Dissecting them alone in a dark room.
It helps to appreciate the narrative,
while eating chips.

Story dynamics of the monster and the virgin sacrifice.
That through the chaotic energies of insufferable evil,
The thing that curbs it all is the death of innocents.
For all the grandeur the hero's bring to slay the beast,
It's the mastery of a little girl that would quell the madness.

And here they are, awed at this story,
stuffing chips in their face.

Yet again, another story permeating the psyche:
The tale of revolutionaries fighting for freedom.
A woman is dying in the leader's arms as battle ensues about them.
A representation of the costs of challenging the system.
She is not the only casualty in the onslaught.

Their ideas of a better world seem to die in that moment.
A moment when there is no undoing these things.
They've made their choice, and the consequences must be paid.
In that climax of the sacrifices one makes for championing an ideal,

They are still stuffing chips in their face.

Complimenting opposites make it exciting.
The rough tough, chagrin male murderer.
A bounty hunter, a soldier, or a gangster.
Offset by a depiction of delicate, soft tones.
The wife, the pacifist, the child.
These make for a compelling narrative.
You need one brawn and one brain;
that no one person is ever both.
A bit of the other maybe,
but not a whole on their own.
It shows how much more we can be when united.

But instead of creating their own story:
They are shoving chips down their throat.

www.ingramcontent.com/pod-product-compliance
Lightning Source LLC
Chambersburg PA
CBHW051747130826
49812CB00033B/1044
9789357449045